RIVER
AND
COAST
GEO FACTS

Izzi Howell

Crabtree Publishing Company
www.crabtreebooks.com

Crabtree Publishing Company
www.crabtreebooks.com
1-800-387-7650

Published in Canada
Crabtree Publishing
616 Welland Avenue
St. Catharines, ON
L2M 5V6

Published in the United States
Crabtree Publishing
PMB 59051
350 Fifth Ave, 59th Floor
New York, NY 10118

Published in 2018 by CRABTREE PUBLISHING COMPANY.

First published in 2017 by The Watts Publishing Group
Copyright © The Watts Publishing Group 2017

Author: Izzi Howell

Editors: Izzi Howell, Ellen Rodger

Design: Rocket Design (East Anglia) Ltd

Editorial director: Kathy Middleton

Proofreader: Angela Kaelberer

Prepress technician: Abigail Smith

Print and production coordinator: Margaret Amy Salter

Photographs

Alamy: Mr. Nut 19tr; iStock: ihsanGercelman 13b, blightylad-infocus 16br, dutchkris 17c, Joanna_Harker 18br, vale_t 21t, menabrea 26t, R.V. Bulck 27c; Peter Bull 4-5; Shutterstock: Tomacco 4t and 14br, Betelgejze 4b, Nicholas Greenaway 5t, Boris Stroujko 5bl, MagSpace 5br, corbac40 6-7c, us1950sr 6bl, Bruno Ismael Silva Alves 6br, Nila Newsom 8l, yakthai 8r, EMJAY SMITH 9t, Travel Stock 9b, ActiveLines 10t, davidsunyol 11l, Iain Frazer 11r, TTstudio 12t, mapichai 12b and 16bl, Dr Morley Read 13t, wickerwood 13c, StockSmartStart 14bl, mariakraynova 15t, Oscity 15b, Photo Image 16t, Thomas Ramsauer 17tl, TTphoto 17tc, 2009fotofriends 17b, Brothers Good 18t, Ulmus Media 18c, tamsindove 18bl, Tony Baggett 19tl, Arndale 19tc, James LePage 19bc, Peter Turner Photography 19b, Designua 20t, Sapsiwai 20b, Mallari 21c, YuriFineart 21b, Panpilas L 22t, Philip Yuan 23t, Production Perig 23c, michaeljung 24, biggunsband 25t, John Grummitt 25b, snapgalleria 27t, Crystal Eye Studio 27b, Lucie Lang 28t, KID_A 29b, PlusONE 29b, Techtype: 8-9, 10b, 14t, 22-23b.

All design elements from Shutterstock: Sentavio, Tako design, Claudia Pylinskaya, Its design, GoodVector, NEILRAS, mire, Evellean, Gabi Wolf, NotionPic, Pulsmusic.

Every attempt has been made to clear copyright. Should there be any inadvertent omission, please apply to the publisher for rectification.

Printed in the USA/122019/BG20171102

Library and Archives Canada Cataloguing in Publication

Howell, Izzi, author
    River and coast geo facts / Izzi Howell.

(Geo facts)
Includes index.
Issued in print and electronic formats.
ISBN 978-0-7787-4393-4 (hardcover).--
ISBN 978-0-7787-4408-5 (softcover).--
ISBN 978-1-4271-2019-9 (HTML)

    1. Rivers--Juvenile literature. 2. Coasts--Juvenile literature. 3. Hydrology--Juvenile literature. 4. Fluvial geomorphology--Juvenile literature. 5. Water--Juvenile literature. 6. Landscape changes--Juvenile literature. I. Title.

GB662.3.H69 2018   j551.48   C2017-906909-8
                                        C2017-906910-1

Library of Congress Cataloging-in Publication Data

Names: Howell, Izzi, author.
Title: River and coast geo facts / Izzi Howell.
Description: New York, New York : Crabtree Publishing, 2018. | Series: Geo facts | Includes index. |
Identifiers: LCCN 2017050657 (print) | LCCN 2017056621 (ebook) | ISBN 9781427120199 (Electronic HTML) | ISBN 9780778743934 (reinforced library binding) | ISBN 9780778744085 (pbk.)
Subjects: LCSH: Rivers--Juvenile literature. | Coasts--Juvenile literature.
Classification: LCC GB1203.8 (ebook) | LCC GB1203.8 .H68 2018 (print) | DDC 551.48/3--dc23
LC record available at https://lccn.loc.gov/2017050657

Contents

Rivers and Coasts

Rivers and coasts are areas where water meets land. Water shapes the landscape in many ways, cutting away narrow mountain streams and wide, curved rivers. It forms rocky cliffs and long sandy beaches along coastlines.

This map shows the main rivers of the world.

 Colorado River (page 14)

FOCUS ON **Venice (page 29)**

Yukon

Mackenzie

Missouri

Colorado

Mississippi

Ni

Amazon

Paraná

Uruguay

Rivers

Channels of freshwater that flow across land are known as rivers. They start in high ground and flow downhill to the ocean. Rivers gain more water as they flow closer to the sea, becoming wider and deeper.

Water cycle

The movement of water from high ground to low ground through rivers is an important part of the **water cycle**. The water cycle is the way in which water moves from Earth's surface to the atmosphere and back again.

 UK coast (page 18)

There are
**221,208 miles
(356,000 km)**
of coastline on Earth.
If you laid out every
coastline in a straight
line, it would almost
reach from Earth
to the Moon!

Coasts

Rough waves and high **tides** carve different landscapes along the coast. The movement and force of water creates many types of coasts, such as beaches and cliffs.

Ob

Yenisei

Amur

Danube

Volga

Yellow

Yangtze

Ganges

Mekong

Nile

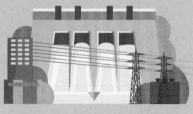

 Three Gorges Dam
(page 26)

Congo

Zambezi

 Ganges River
(page 8)

Darling

Murray

Twelve Apostles
(page 23)

River Structure

Rivers start out in high areas as narrow, fast-flowing streams. They become wider and slower as they move downhill toward the sea.

Source

The **source** is the place where a river starts. Rivers can begin as springs, where water comes to the surface from deep underground. Some emerge as tiny streams of water from melted **glaciers** or pools of rainwater, which run downhill.

Finding a source

It can be difficult to decide exactly where a river begins. In some cases, there are many small streams that all flow into the same large river. Geographers usually consider the source to be the furthest point upstream on the longest **tributary**. Tributaries are small streams or rivers that flow into larger rivers.

Some rivers begin in damp, boggy marshlands. In these cases, the highest part of the marshland is considered the source of the river.

Upper course

Near the source, rivers do not contain much water. They are narrow, shallow channels that flow quickly downhill. This stage is known as the upper course.

6

Middle course

In the middle course, rivers slow down as they flow over flatter ground. Tributaries join the river and add more water to it. This makes the river wider. As the river flows over the ground, it picks up **sediment** that makes the water murkier.

Lakes

Some water that falls to the ground also drains into lakes. Unlike rivers, the water in these lakes is calmer. Many lakes have connecting rivers, although some are totally isolated.

Lower course

Rivers slow down and become wider as they cross flat ground. This stage is called the lower course. Rivers are often very deep in the lower course.

River basins

When it rains, water that falls to the ground flows overland or underground toward a river. The area of land that is drained by a river is known as a river basin. This water is then carried to the sea by the river as part of the water cycle.

The Amazon River has the largest river basin on Earth. Around
20 percent
of all water carried to the ocean by rivers is carried by the Amazon River.

Mouth

The mouth of the River Minho in northern Portugal marks the border between Spain and Portugal.

The place where a river meets the ocean (or a lake) is known as its mouth. All of the water from the river empties into the ocean or a lake. When rivers empty into the ocean, they create a mixture of freshwater and salt water in the area around the mouth.

FOCUS ON

The Ganges River

The Ganges River flows from its source high in the Himalayas down to the coast of India and Bangladesh. It is one of the most important rivers in India.

FACT FILE

LENGTH
1,559 miles (2,510 km)

AVERAGE DISCHARGE
388,461 cubic feet per second (11,000 cubic m/per sec.)

COUNTRIES
India, Bangladesh

Several sources

Stories in **Hindu** mythology say that the Bhagirathi River is the **holy** source stream of the Ganges River. Geographers consider the Alaknanda River to be its true source. This is because the Alaknanda River is longer and contributes more water to the Ganges. Both rivers flow from glaciers in the Himalayas.

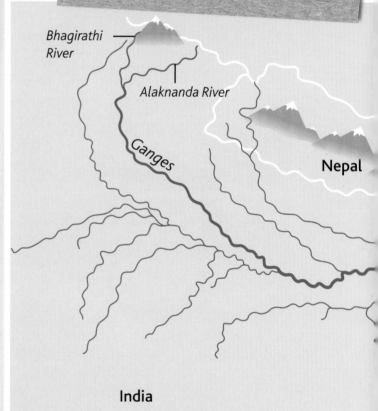

Bhagirathi River

Alaknanda River

Ganges

Nepal

India

The source of the Bhagirathi River is known as Gaumukh, which means cow's mouth in Hindi, a widely-spoken Indian language. People believe that the tip of the glacier resembles a cow's mouth.

Beginning of the Ganges

The meeting point of the Alaknanda River and the Bhagirathi River is where the river becomes known as the Ganges. The narrow Ganges flows through the valleys of the outer **Himalayas** in its upper course.

This is the place where the two rivers meet and become known as the Ganges.

Plains

In northern India, the Ganges flows across a massive plain of fertile land, or land where crops grown well. Many other rivers cross this plain, including the large Indus River. As the Ganges flows southeast, it is joined by tributaries that bring more water to the river. The extra water makes the Ganges wider and slower.

China

Bhutan

Ganges

Bangladesh

Ganges Delta

In its lower course, the Ganges splits into many smaller rivers as it flows into the sea. This formation is known as a **delta** (see page 13). The Ganges Delta is one of the largest in the world. Narrow river channels flow between swamps, lakes, and **mangroves**. Many crops, such as rice, are grown in the fertile delta soil.

Hundreds of millions of people live in the Ganges river basin. Many towns dump *sewage* and garbage into the river, making it the fifth most polluted river in the world.

A holy river

The Ganges is a sacred, or holy, river for Hindus. People travel across India to bathe in its waters and float flowers and candles on it. Many Hindu festivals are held on its banks.

Some Hindus bathe in the Ganges every day as a religious ritual.

River Erosion

Over millions of years, the movement of rivers gradually shapes the landscape. Rivers change the land by **eroding** rock, or carrying rocks along and leaving them downstream.

Eroding rock

Water erodes rock in four different ways. These methods of erosion are explained in the diagrams below.

Some types of soft rock and soil dissolve in water.

When water gets into cracks in the river bank, it widens the crack and the rock eventually breaks away.

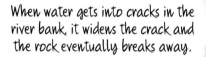

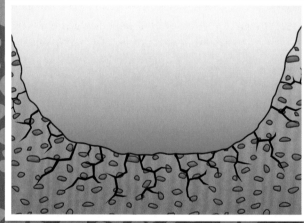

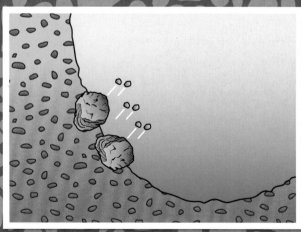

Rocks that have fallen into the river chip away at the river bank.

Rocks carried by the river smash into each other and break down into smaller pieces. These tiny pieces of rock float in the river as sediment.

Load

When a river is moving fast, it has enough energy to carry material such as rocks and pebbles. This material is known as a river's load. Large rocks carried by a river sink to the bottom and roll along the river bed. Small rocks are carried nearer the surface.

The fast-moving water in the upper course of the Blue Nile, one of the tributaries of the Nile, breaks away jagged rocks from the river banks.

Vertical erosion

In the upper course, rivers erode vertically and cut channels into the land. They carry rough rocks that bounce up and down in the water and deepen the river bed.

Horizontal erosion

In the middle and lower course, rivers erode horizontally and become wider. The river's load of smaller, smooth rocks floats near the surface and erodes the river banks.

Leaving rock behind

As a river grows in size, it slows down and loses energy. It drops its **load** as it slows down in the middle course, as it no longer has the energy to carry it. First, it drops the largest, heaviest rocks. Finally, it drops tiny particles of sediment.

The stones left behind on this river bank in the middle course have been smoothed by the flowing water.

River Formations

As a river travels along its course, it shapes the surrounding landscape. Different features can be seen at each part of a river's course.

Waterfalls and gorges

In the upper course, rivers often flow over different kinds of rock. Soft rock is eroded more quickly than hard rock. The movement of rivers over soft and hard rock creates waterfalls and **gorges**.

*The **plunge pool** at the base of the Seljalandsfoss waterfall in Iceland has eroded a small cave behind the waterfall.*

! Less than 0.3 percent of the freshwater on Earth is found in rivers, and yet they have a dramatic impact on our landscape.

Angel Falls waterfall in Venezuela is so high that some falling water evaporates before it hits the plunge pool.

1. Soft rock is worn away by the movement of the river.

2. Hard rock, which takes longer to erode, is left hanging over the soft rock.

3. The unsupported hard rock falls away.

4. The fallen rocks swirl around at the base of the waterfall and cut into the hard rock, eroding it further.

5. Over time, the waterfall cuts away more rock, creating a steep-sided gorge.

12

The river flows fastest on the outside bend, washing away the river bank.

The slow moving water on the inner bend doesn't have enough energy to carry its load. It drops sediment and rocks inside the bend.

The Amazon River creates winding meanders through the Amazon rain forest.

Meanders

Rivers often have meanders (bends) in their middle and lower courses. Meanders are caused by bands of hard rock, which rivers swerve to avoid. Over time, meanders slowly move and change shape. This is because of the way the water flows around the bends.

These drawings show how an oxbow lake is formed.

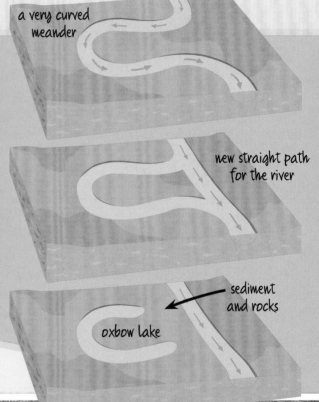

a very curved meander

new straight path for the river

sediment and rocks

oxbow lake

Oxbow lake

A meander that is cut off from the rest of the river is known an oxbow lake. If a meander is very curved, the river may cut across, making a new straight channel. Sediment and rocks build up on the side of the river, cutting off the oxbow lake.

Deltas

Rivers drop sediment when they reach the sea, as the slow-moving water does not have enough energy to carry its load any longer. This sediment can block the river. The water is diverted around the sediment and splits into a fan of smaller streams called a delta.

This is the delta of the Dalyan River in Turkey. It flows into the Mediterranean Sea.

sediment

The Colorado River

The Colorado River flows across the southwest of the US and Mexico. It has created stunning rock formations along its 1,450-mile-long (2,334 km) course.

FACT FILE

LENGTH
1,450 miles (2,334 km)

AVERAGE DISCHARGE
22,496 cubic feet per second (637 cubic m per sec.)

COUNTRIES
USA, Mexico

Course

The Colorado River begins high in the Rocky Mountains. In its middle course, it crosses the Colorado Plateau, home to the Grand Canyon. It fans out into a delta as it reaches its mouth on the west coast of Mexico.

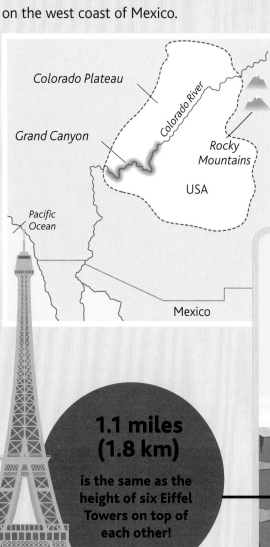

Colorado Plateau

Grand Canyon

Colorado River

Rocky Mountains

USA

Pacific Ocean

Mexico

Colorado Plateau

A plateau is a large, flat, high area of land. The Colorado Plateau was created billions of years ago by moving pieces of Earth's crust (plates). When the plates collided and moved over each other, they formed the Colorado Plateau and the Rocky Mountains.

Grand Canyon

The Colorado River flows through the Grand Canyon—a massive, steep-sided canyon in Arizona. In some places, it is up to 18 miles (29 km) wide and over 1.1 miles (1.8 km) deep. It is one of the most famous landscapes in the world.

1.1 miles (1.8 km) is the same as the height of six Eiffel Towers on top of each other!

Making a canyon

Scientists aren't exactly sure when the Grand Canyon was created or how it became so huge. Some think that the rising of the plateau, caused by moving plates, made the flowing Colorado River cut down even further into the rock. The width of the canyon is probably a result of **landslides** and erosion caused by small side streams.

Horseshoe Bend gets its name from the horseshoe shape of its meander.

Horseshoe Bend

In its middle course, the Colorado River has a meander named Horseshoe Bend. Unlike most meanders, the steep canyon walls trap the river so that it can't take an easier route. Eventually, the water could erode through the rock between the meander, making a bridge or even an oxbow lake.

Rainbow Bridge has been a sacred place for Indigenous peoples for centuries.

Rainbow Bridge

This magnificent rainbow-shaped natural bridge was created by a tributary of the Colorado River. At first, the river meandered around the side of the bridge. Then, the river changed course and eroded a hole through the rock, creating a natural bridge.

Types of Coasts

Coasts are areas where the ocean meets the land. There are many types of coasts, such as beaches, cliffs, and salt marshes.

Beaches

When pieces of rock wash up on the coast, a beach is formed. The sand on beaches is actually very small pieces of rock. Larger rocks form pebbly beaches. Low waves carry pebbles and sand up the beach. Strong, tall waves drag rocks down the beach and back into the sea.

This beach on the island of Hawaii has black sand. The sand comes from black volcanic rock that has been broken down into sand by the movement of the sea.

Cliffs

In some places, the land dramatically cuts away along the coast, forming almost upright cliffs. Cliffs are created by waves hitting rock at **sea level**. Over time, this rock wears away, leaving the rock above without any support. Eventually, the top of the cliff falls into the sea, leaving a upright slope.

Some seabirds build their nests on cliffs. The sheer slope of the cliffs makes it very difficult for predators to attack the nest. The birds fly in and out easily!

Dunes

The low hills of sand that form inland from beaches are known as dunes. They are caused by wind pushing sand inland. Dunes help to protect against flooding during very high tides as the sand acts as a barrier against the water. Plants that grow in the salty sand create an important habitat for many animals.

The roots and stems of marram grass keep sand dunes from blowing away.

Sea holly can survive being buried in sand.

Tides

Most coastlines change with the tides. At high tide, the level of water rises and covers land at **sea level**. At low tide, the water level drops, and the coastline is exposed again. Tides happen because **gravity** from the Moon and the Sun pulls on Earth.

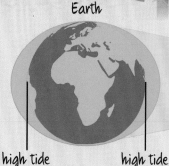

Earth

Moon

gravitational force of the Moon

high tide   high tide

The pull of the Moon's gravity on Earth makes the oceans bulge slightly, creating tides.

Some beaches have rock pools, which fill with saltwater and small sea animals at high tide. The water and animals remain in the pools at low tide.

Salt marsh

At high tide, sea water covers salt marshes. These are muddy areas of land along the coast that are covered in small plants. The plants in salt marshes can survive in saltwater, unlike most other plants. Salt marshes are often found near **estuaries**.

The UK Coast

The United Kingdom has nearly 7,767 miles (12,500 km) of coastline. In different areas of the country, the coastline changes dramatically.

Loch Etive

Loch Etive is a sea inlet on the west coast of Scotland formed by an ancient glacier. A loch is a lake, or a long, narrow arm of the sea. The glacier melted and left a deep channel with steep cliffs on either side. Before and after high spring tides, fast-moving rapids form at the place where the loch joins the open ocean.

Giant's Causeway

Found on the north coast of Northern Ireland, this stunning rock formation was caused by an ancient volcanic eruption. When the volcano erupted, it covered the chalk landscape with layers of basalt, or volcanic rock. As the basalt cooled, it contracted and cracked, forming honeycomb-shaped pillars.

Morecambe Bay

There are several estuaries in northwest England, but at 120 square miles (310 square km), Morecambe Bay is the largest. At low tide, you can walk across the **mudflats** and sand to islands in jthe bay. The bay can be dangerous, as the tide comes in quickly.

Rhossili Bay

Many consider Rhossili Bay to be one of the best beaches in Europe. Its three miles (five km) of golden sandy beach makes it a very popular tourist attraction, bringing many visitors to the south coast of Wales every year.

Spurn Head Spit

Spurn Head Spit is in Yorkshire, northern England. A spit is a long piece of land that juts into the ocean. The Spurn Head Spit was formed when waves washed sand and sediment to the coast. The wave action makes the spit grow longer each year.

Seven Sisters

These iconic white cliffs on the southeast coast of England are made from a soft rock called chalk. The cliffs crack easily, and large chunks often fall away, leaving behind sheer cliff faces.

! *The Seven Sisters are eroding by 12 to 15 inches (30-38 cm) every year! Some houses built close to the cliff edge are at risk of falling over the cliff.*

Braunton Burrows

The largest area of sand dunes in Europe is found on the north coast of Devon. Braunton Burrows is home to over 400 different species of plants, including many types of lichen.

Changing Coasts

Waves change the shape of coasts through erosion. Water breaks away rock and brings it onto land again, creating new formations.

Waves

Waves are caused by wind blowing across the surface of the water. The wind transfers energy to the water, which makes the water move in a circle. It is this energy, rather than the water, that travels across the ocean.

wind

circular movement of water

Coastal erosion

Every few seconds, waves crash onto the land. The force and weight of the water puts pressure on the rock. Over time, the rock shatters into smaller pieces and falls away into the water. Waves also carry small rocks that smash into the coastline, eroding it further.

Large, powerful waves erode cliffs faster than low, gentle waves.

Rock

Coasts are made of hard rock, soft rock, or a mixture of both. Sand and clay are examples of soft rocks, while granite is a hard rock. Soft rock is eroded by waves more quickly than hard rock.

Bays and headlands

When areas of soft rock are eroded, it creates a bay, which has land on three sides. The hard rock at the sides of a bay is left sticking out, as it erodes more slowly. This is known as a headland.

bay   headland

These bays and headlands are on the coast of New Zealand. Headlands and bays have water on three sides.

Longshore drift

The direction of the wind makes waves hit the coast at an angle. This means that the sand and pebbles carried by the waves are also brought onto the beach at an angle. After a wave breaks, the water flows straight back down to the sea. This zigzag movement of water moves large amounts of sand and pebbles along the beach.

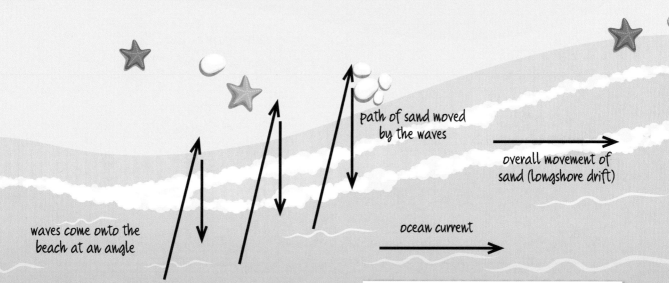

path of sand moved by the waves

overall movement of sand (longshore drift)

waves come onto the beach at an angle

ocean current

Protection

There are several ways to protect coastlines against erosion. Placing large rocks at the base of a cliff stops waves from hitting and eroding the cliff itself. Building **groins** on beaches reduces the effects of longshore drift. The groins stop sand and pebbles from moving along the coastline.

Longshore drift has caused a large amount of sand to build up on the right side of this groin.

Arches and Stacks

Coastal erosion can create dramatic sea caves, arches, and stacks. This process takes many years, but strong waves or storms can erode things faster.

Caves

When waves hit a crack in the rock of a headland, the water puts pressure on the crack and opens it further. Over time, the waves erode the crack further, and it develops into a sea cave.

! Sometimes, the roof of a sea cave can collapse, leaving behind a large hole. This hole on the west coast of the United States is known as the Devil's Punch Bowl.

Arches

The movement of waves hitting the walls of the sea cave continues to erode the rock. Eventually, water will break through to the other side of the headland. This creates an arch.

Stack

Sooner or later, the unsupported weight of the arch will make it collapse. A tall stack is left behind. Waves hitting the top of the stack will erode it into a stump.

This is how sea caves, arches, and stacks are formed.

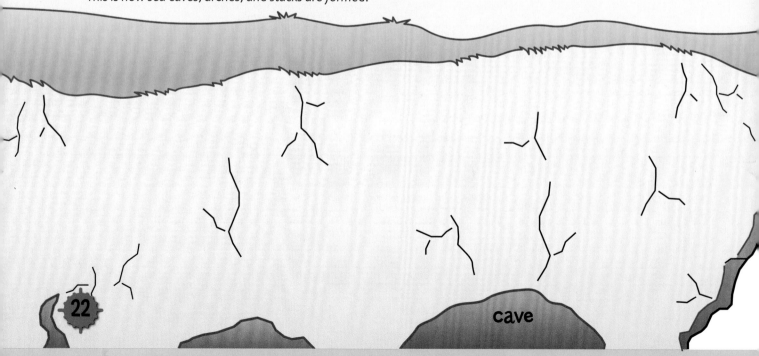

cave

FOCUS ON

The Twelve Apostles

The Twelve Apostles are a magnificent rock formation on the south coast of Australia. Until 2005, there were nine stacks. Today, only eight remain.

Each stack has eroded differently, resulting in a range of different shapes.

Stages of erosion

The cliffs that make up the Twelve Apostles are in different stages of the erosion process. The main stacks are now far from the cliff and will eventually wear away into short stumps before disappearing entirely. Nearby, there are caves and arches. One day, these will erode and replace the original stacks.

From above, you can see many different stages in the erosion process across the Twelve Apostles. The rock formations are constantly changing.

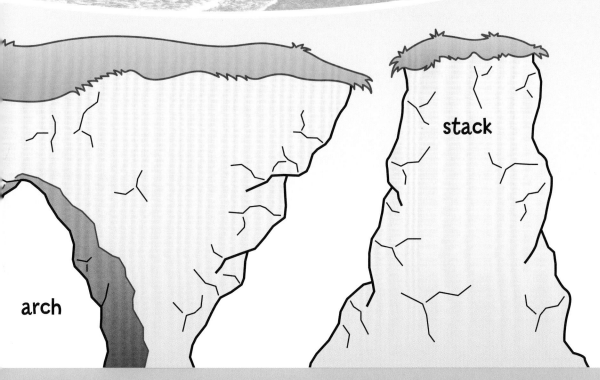

arch

stack

stump

People and Water

People have always built **settlements** by coasts and rivers. They depended on water for transportation and fishing. Today, rivers and coasts are still important for many industries.

Cities

Some of the largest cities in the world, including Shanghai in China, Lagos in Nigeria, and New York City in the United States, were built along coastlines. Many cities are also found on rivers, such as London, England and Chicago. These cities became successful and grew in size due to the money brought in by trade ships.

Cape Town in South Africa grew from a small settlement to a large city, thanks to the wealth of traders who stopped off there on their way from the Indian Ocean to the Atlantic Ocean.

Today, around **40 percent** of the world's population lives within 62 miles (100 km) of the coast.

Tourism

Rivers and coasts are popular tourist destinations, due to their natural beauty and the activities they offer. Sandy beaches are the perfect place for a relaxing vacation, while adventurous people can enjoy windsurfing, snorkeling, or water skiing.

Industry

Many factories and power plants are located along rivers and coasts. Some use the moving water from the river to turn turbines and make energy. Others use water to cool down the hot steam that is created during the process of making electricity.

Pollution

Humans can have a negative impact on rivers and coasts by polluting them with garbage, chemicals, and sewage. This kills plants and animals that live in the water. It can also be dangerous for those who get their drinking water from rivers.

Ports and harbors

Ships of all sizes come to ports to load and unload goods. Ports are often built in harbors. Harbors are areas of water near the coast that have walls to protect ships from the rough waves of the open ocean. Some harbors have artificial walls, while others are in natural inlets that are protected by land.

The harbor in Dubrovnik, Croatia, is surrounded by stone walls. Ships shelter in the harbor when they are not in use.

New land

In areas without much land to build on, land can be reclaimed from the sea or from floodplains. This is done by placing earth and stones into the water until the land is above sea level.

Nearly **one-sixth** of the land in the Netherlands is reclaimed land!

These excavators, or diggers, are building up layers of sand on an area that is being reclaimed from the sea in Saudi Arabia.

FOCUS ON

The Three Gorges Dam

The Three Gorges Dam is a **hydroelectric dam** on the Yangtze River in China. It uses water from the river to produce electricity. The dam is one of the largest power stations in the world.

Structure

Only a limited amount of water can flow through the Three Gorges Dam. The rest of the water from the Yangtze River is trapped in a **reservoir** behind the dam.

The Three Gorges Dam is over 1.2 miles (2 km) wide and 606 feet (185 m) tall.

Ships

The Three Gorges Dam is built in the middle course of the Yangtze. Before the construction of the dam, the river in this area was fairly wide and deep, but not deep enough for large container ships. Now, these ships can easily travel through the deep water in the reservoir, bringing goods further up the river.

Reservoir

Yangtze River

Three Gorges Dam

Flooding

As well as producing electricity, the dam also controls and reduces flooding along the Yangtze. Before the construction of the dam, people who lived along the Yangtze suffered severe flooding. Over 300,000 people were killed by flooding along the Yangtze in the 1900s alone.

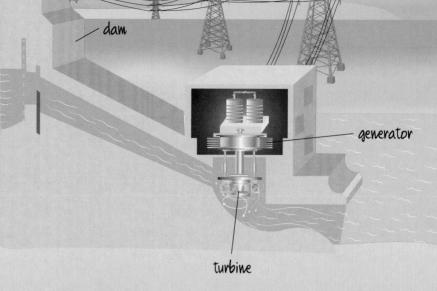

How it works

reservoir

dam

generator

turbine

When water from the reservoir flows through the small gap in the dam wall, it pushes down on turbines and makes them spin. These turbines are connected to a generator. The generator works as a motor and produces electricity. Using hydroelectric dams is a **sustainable** way of generating electricity. We will never run out of water to power the generators.

Making the dam

The Three Gorges Dam is built in an area of the Yangtze known for its three dramatic gorges. The gorges, along with many towns, villages, and historical sites, were deliberately flooded during the construction of the Three Gorges Dam. Many people lost their homes.

The sheer sides of the Three Gorges now appear shorter because of the higher water level caused by flooding.

Threats and problems

The high level of water in the reservoir behind the dam causes severe erosion and landslides. Downstream, some areas are suffering from drought as they receive much less water than before.

Flooding

A flood happens when the water level rises and water comes onto land that is normally dry. Floods can affect banks and coasts of rivers, lakes, and oceans.

This river in the UK has overflowed its banks, flooding a path and benches alongside it.

River floods

Snow that has melted upstream or heavy rains can increase the amount of water in a river. When the level of water in a river rises above the banks, the river will flood.

Flash floods

Floods that appear suddenly are known as flash floods. These happen when rain falls so hard and fast that the land can't absorb it. Flash floods are common in dry areas or in cities, where water can't be absorbed by land or concrete and storm sewers can't handle the flow.

Benefits

When a river floods, it leaves behind muddy sediment on the land. This mud fertilizes the land on the floodplain and makes it great for growing crops. Many ancient civilizations, such as the ancient Egyptians, depended on flooding to fertilize their farmland.

Coastal floods

Areas along the coast sometimes experience flooding during storms, when large waves are pushed onto land by strong winds. If these storms happen at the same time as a high tide, the flooding can be even worse.

Tsunamis are giant waves that cause extreme flooding and destroy anything in their path. Tsunami waves can measure up to **197 feet (60 m) high.**

Protection

We can reduce the risk of flooding by building dams in rivers to control the water flow. Sea walls can be built along the coast to stop strong waves from coming onto land. If these options fail, flood warning systems help alert people in time so that they can escape from danger.

FOCUS ON Venice

The city of Venice, Italy, is built on several islands in a coastal **lagoon**. It regularly experiences floods.

Causes

Venice's flooding problem is caused by rising sea levels and the gradual sinking of the land beneath the city. The floods in Venice are known as *acqua alta* and mainly happen in winter, during high tides.

Tourists continue to visit Venice, in spite of the flooding.

Barriers

If left uncontrolled, Venice's flooding could threaten the future of the city. However, the Italian government is in the final stages of completing a flood barrier around Venice. This barrier will be able to stop tides of up to 9.8 feet (3 m).

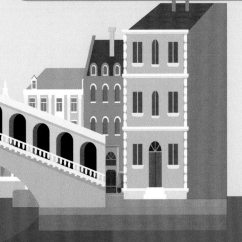

Glossary

delta An area of low land where a river splits into several small streams before flowing into the sea

erode Gradually wear away rock or land

estuary The wide part of a river where it joins the sea

glacier A mass of ice formed over many years that moves slowly

gorge A deep, narrow valley with steep sides

gravity The Force that attracts, or pulls, an object toward a body, such as a planet, that has a large mass

groin A low wall built on a coast to stop the waves moving sand and rocks along the beach

Himalayas A mountain range in Asia that includes Mount Everest, the world's highest

Hindu A person who follows Hinduism, a belief system that originated in South Asia

holy Something considered sacred or godly in a religion or belief system

hydroelectric dam A wall built across a river that controls the flow of the water and uses it to make electricity

lagoon An area of sea water separated from the sea by a barrier

landslide The movement of rocks and earth down a steep slope

load The rocks and sediment carried by water

mangroves Trees and shrubs that grow in tropical marshes

mudflat A flat area of mud that is covered by water at high tide

plunge pool Water at the bottom of a waterfall

reservoir A place where water is stored

sea level The height of the sea where it meets the land

sediment Very small pieces of rock and natural materials that are carried in water

settlement A place where humans have settled and live permanently, such as a town

sewage Waste matter, such as urine

source The place where a river starts

sustainable Something that is capable of being supported or maintained

tide The rise and fall of the sea that happens every day

tributary A river or stream that flows into another river

water cycle The way in which water moves from Earth's surface to the atmosphere and back again

Test yourself!

1 Which river has the largest river basin on Earth?

2 Which religion considers the Ganges to be a holy river?

3 In which part of the course do rivers erode vertically?

4 What is another name for a meander that has been cut off from the rest of the river?

5 How can dunes protect coasts from flooding?

6 Name two cities that are built on rivers.

7 Name one advantage and one disadvantage of the Three Gorges Dam.

8 When do floods usually happen in Venice?

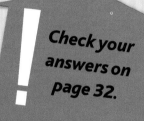

Check your answers on page 32.

Further reading

Rivers Around the World series
(Crabtree, 2010)

Ecosystems Research Journal series
(Crabtree, 2018)

Ecosystems Inside Out series
(Crabtree, 2015)

Websites

Read more about rivers and coasts at the following websites:

kids.britannica.com/elementary/article-476241/coast?

www.bbc.co.uk/schools/riversandcoasts/rivers/whatis_river/

www.theschoolrun.com/homework-help/rivers

Index

Answers

1 The Amazon River

2 The Hindu religion

3 The upper course

4 An oxbow lake

5 The sand acts as a barrier to stop the water coming onto the land.

6 Some cities include London, Chicago, and Paris.

7 Some advantages include producing sustainable energy and reducing flooding along the Yangtze. Some disadvantages include flooding during construction, landslides in the reservoir, and droughts downstream.

8 In winter, during high tides.